Ethnographic Profile of Adiya Tribe, Kerala.

MODERNIZATION AND ACCULTURATION AMONG ADIYA TRIBAL COMMUNITIES OF THRISSILERY VILLAGE, WAYANAD

Junaid KC & Divya NV

ISBN: 9798723362451

DEDICATION

This book is dedicated to our teacher,
Dr. Jesurathnam Devarapalli, Pondicherry University.

CONTENTS

ACKNOWLEDGMENTS

We would like to thank all Adiya community members of Thrissilery Village, Wayanad (Kerala) for their cooperation during fieldwork. We thank our Parents, Friends and Colleagues for their support and everyone who has helped directly and indirectly during the fieldwork.

1

INTRODUCTION

According to the 2011 census of India, there are 645 distinct Tribal groups in India with 104 million population, of which around 90% lives in rural areas and 10% in urban areas. Tribal communities have been influenced by many factors like Colonisation, Industrialization, Modernisation, Globalisation and Digitalisation in India. Tribes in India are portrayed by extraordinary heterogeneity, being put at various dimensions of social and financial development. Everyone has responded differently to the forces of change. Some have progressed others have become devastated as they interacted with the modernized societies and social systems. Conversely, some change with factors of modernization. The same has reflected in aspects of modernization and acculturation among Adiya tribal communities of Kerala too. To understand the matter deeply the authors have conducted an ethnographic study on Adiya tribal communities in Thrissilery village of Wayanad district in Kerala. Moreover to the Socio-Cultural, Economical, Physical, and Psychological aspects of life, the book tries to discuss different dimensions of modernization and acculturation. Modernization among the Adiya tribe has started from long back. First, the colonization brought some changes to their culture and work system. Later interaction of Non-Tribals made few changes especially religious and food systems. Then the governments and other non-government agents influenced the Adiya to change different aspects of life like Health care, Education, Religion and Economy. Now change is happening because of Technological advancements and Digitalisation. Overall Modernization and different agents of modernization on Adiya communities made them be in the Detribalization process. Likewise, Acculturation took place in the tribal culture of Kerala also. Many studies have highlighted that the rate of acculturation is more among the Paniya, Kurichia, and Adiya tribes of Kerala. Trends and reasons of acculturation among the Adiya tribes with special reference to the Adiya tribes of Kerala are discussed in this book. The role of acculturation in the culture change of Adiya tribes of Thrissilery village is very evident. It can be dated back to the colonial period of India, starting from the Economic organization and occupational change acculturation took place in almost all walks of their life, and it continues. The influence of non-tribal groups, other tribes, tribal development programmes, transportation and communication facilities, education etc. are the major reasons for these changes. Overall, the authors have tried to illustrate an extensive ethnographic profile of Adiya tribes in Kerala with dimensions of modernization and acculturation.

2

ETHNOGRAPHIC PROFILE OF ADIYA TRIBE

Introduction
History
Environmental Conditions
Physical Feature, Ornaments and Dress
Language
Food Habits
Family Structure and Clans
Marriage System
Kinship System
Occupation and Economic Organization
Religion, Rituals and Customs
Traditional Art Forms

2.1 Introduction

KERALA AND TRIBE

Kerala situated on the southwestern, Coast of India (Malabar Cost). Officially recognized as a state on 1 November 1956, after the States Reorganization Act, by joining Malayalam speaking area together. Kerala is the twenty-second Indian state with a size of 38,863 km2. It is circumscribed by Karnataka toward the upper east, Tamil Nadu toward the east and south, and the Lakshadweep Sea and North Arabian Sea toward the west. According to the 2018 survey Kerala has 34,742,592 (3.47 Crore) people with a sex ratio of 1084 females per 1,000 males. Kerala is separated into 14 regions with the capital being Thiruvananthapuram. Malayalam is the official state language and also Kerala is known as the "God's Own Country".

As the tribal population is an important social segment of India, Kerala does have this representation. In the Malayalam language also Tribe is called 'Adivasi', which means aboriginal people. The majority of the indigenous peoples of Kerala lives in the forests and heaps of the Western Ghats, which shares a border with Karnataka and Tamil Nadu. According to 2011 registration, Kerala has a population 4,84,839 (1.45 percent) Adivasi communities. Adivasis who are food gatherers, with lessening their numbers and low literacy and economic rates can be termed as Particularly Vulnerable Tribal Groups (PVTG). Kattunaikans, Cholanaikkans, Kadars, Kurumbas, and Koragas are the five primitive tribal groups in Kerala. They account for almost 5% of the total tribal population in the State. Cholanaikkans are the most primitive found in the Malappuram District. Just a bunch of families are living in the Mancheri slopes of the Nilambur forest division. Kattunaikans, another hill tribe identified with Cholanaikkans, are fundamentally observed in the Wayanad region and some in Malappuram and Kozhikode. Kadar populace is found in Thrissur and Palakkad areas. Kurumbas are living in the Attappady Block of Palakkad locale. The Koraga people's natural habitat is in the plain territories of the Kasaragod area.

WAYANAD AND TRIBE

Wayanad district is located in the north-east of Kerala with district headquarters at Kalpetta. Situated in the Western Ghats with heights ranging from 700 to 2100. The locale was shaped on 1 November 1980 as the twelfth region in Kerala via cutting out regions from

Kozhikode and Kannur regions. About 885.92.sq.km of the territory of the locale is under forest cover. Wayanad has three municipalities Kalpetta, Mananthavady and Sulthan Bathery. There are numerous tribes around there. Wayanad area is bordered by Karnataka to north and north-east, Tamil Nadu to the south-east, Malappuram to south, Kozhikode to south-west and Kannur to the north-west. The caves of Ambukuthimala and different conformations expresses that the spot is as old as the start of the New Age Civilisation. The tribal belt of Wayanad has been the natural abode for some of the ethnic groups like Adiya, Kurichia, Paniyas, Kattunayakan, Kurumas, Ooralis, Uraali Kurumas etc.

ADIYA TRIBE AND THRISSILERY VILLAGE

In Kerala, the Adiya tribal communities are mainly distributed in the Mananthavady taluk of the Wayanad district and are also seen in other regions like Kannur. About 99 per cent of the Adiyan populace is settled in Wayanad District only. However, a few families have proceeded in their migration to Kozhikode, Kottayam, Idukki, and Ernakulam Districts. In Wayanad District, Adiyans are scattered in 9 Grama Panchayats, particularly in Thirunelly, Mananthavady, Panamaram and Pulpally. Out of these 45.35 per cent of the Adiya tribe are in Thirunelli Grama Panchayat of Mananthavady taluk. They were part of the bonded labour system until the 1970-the 80s and were landless and agricultural labourers. Now they live in harmony with different religious people around them. The Adiya is originally migrated from Coorg (Karnataka). As per the elders, they practised nomadism and that's how they reached Wayanad from Coorg. As the name shows, they were the reinforced workers of landlords. They are customarily known as Ravulayar or Ravula tribe. And the tribal network is isolated into 20 classes called Mandu. The leader of the Mandu is called Chemmakkaran or Peruman. The 'Nattumoopan' or 'Peruman' controls the territorial undertakings of the network. 'Gadhika' or 'Gadhika' is a well-known fine art of the Adiya people. The Adiya tribal females are specialists in body tattooing, while females tattoo on face and males in hand. Tribe songs known as Sopanappattu and Poigavanappattu are extremely well known. They have Thudi (drum) and Cheeni (flute) as their vital melodic instruments. 'Gadhikamadal' is a customary dance type of Adiya and they trust that the Gadhika dancer has superhuman powers to cure diseases. They have a place with Hindu religion and love Hindu divine beings like Mariamman, Kali, Bhadrakali, Bhagavathy, Valluramma, Chikkamma, Kariyathan, Mallappan, Adili Sasuvappan as their deities. Without gender and age difference they used to chew betel leaves. Adiyans have a habit of chewing betel leaves with areca nut, slaked lime, and it in Tobacco. As Adiya is practising matrilineal systems, female family names are followed generation after generation. Adiya is in the Detribalisation process in the current times. Kurichya, Kurumba and Kattunayakan are the other scheduled tribe lives along with the Adiya people in the 16th ward of Thrissilery Village. Other than these scheduled tribe, Non-tribal groups like Muslim, Hindu and Christians are also there. The interaction between all these groups influences the lives of each other. Sometimes Adiya people are depending on Kurichia for honey and other forest products like medicinal plants etc. because Adiya of these colonies is not going into the inner forest for collecting forest products. Not only do they need the help of Kurichia, but they also buy bamboo products from the Kurumba tribe. Kattunayakan and Adiya people are not having much interaction because their houses are far from the Adiya colony and only 4-5 households are there. Compared to Adiya tribal population in the 16th ward, Kurumba and Kurichia are less in number. Many Adiya people are working in other fields as daily wage labourers. The local shops in both Varinilam and Kaithavally colony are managed by non-tribe. Among the tribal groups in this ward Kurichia claims to be superior to other tribes in the colony, and they are the most developed tribal group in the ward.

2.2 History

Adiya people call themselves Ravular, people who speak the Ravula language. The Ravula language itself has a connection with the language of the Yerava tribe of neighbouring state Karnataka, and they consider themselves as migrants from Karnataka to Kerala. According to them the meaning of the word Ravular is travellers, and traditionally they were nomads. They travel from one place to another as small bands along with cattle. Adiya are settled in different parts of Wayanad district including Thrissilery before 10 generations and become the inhabitants of Kerala. During that period they were forced to work under the landlords as bonded labour and their name changed to Adiya from Ravular. Their name is reported to have originated from an old rule that they should maintain a distance of 'ar' (six), 'adi' (feet) to avoid pollution (Luiz, 1962: 27). And they become the Adiya Tribe. The meaning of the word Adiya is 'Slave' in Malayalam and was treated as slaves by the landlord. They were freed from bonded labour by the 1976 Bonded Labour (abolition) Act. Landlords and the bonded labour system have an important role in the life and history of these colonies. The names of the colonies were changed because of landlords. Before the arrival of landlords Kaithavally Colony was known as Elikkuni, Chekkot Colony as Kalakkara and Varinilam Colony as Polakkulam. Name Kaithavally Colony is the house name of the landlord of Elikkuni, and later the colony itself became Kaithavally.

2.3 Environmental Conditions

Wayanad, green heaven settled among mountains of the Western Ghats, is one of the best hill stations of Kerala. Situated at a distance of 76 Kms from the seashores of Kozhikode, this quiet land lies at a height of 700-2100 m above ocean level. It is one of the greatest foreign exchange contributors to the state on account of its money harvests of pepper, cardamom, coffee, tea and other spices. As the name proposes Wayanad (Wayal Nadu) is the place where there are paddy fields, one can see tremendous territories of paddy fields here. Farming in Wayanad is similarly partitioned among paddy and major crops. Because of the impossible to miss territory, there are east streaming and west streaming waterways. The low slopes are brimming with major crops like tea, coffee, pepper and cardamom while valleys have the power of paddy fields. Thrissilery has the same environmental conditions as any other location in Wayanad. The highest and lowest temperature throughout the previous five years was 29 degree Celsius and 18 degree Celsius respectively. This spot encounters high relative dampness which goes even up to 95 per cent amid the south-west monsoon. By and large, the year is classified into four seasons, in particular, Cold climate (December-February), Hot climate (March-May), south-west rainy season (June-September) and the northeast rainy season (October-November). Flora and Fauna include Careya Arborea (Pezhu), Kydia calycina (Vellachadachi), Dalbergia latifolia (Rosewood), Termination chebula (Kadukka), Anogeissus latifolia (Axle wood), Stereospermum colais (Padiri) etc. are the dominant tree species. Different kinds of shrubs are locally available in this area.

Wild animals like Elephant, Tiger, Peacock and monkey are common in nearby forest regions. Honey Bees, squirrel, Wild hen etc are also seen. Adiya possesses domestic animals like Cows, Buffaloes, Goats and Dogs. Kitchen gardens with a wide variety of vegetables are promoted by the Kudumbashree units. Vegetables like cabbage, cauliflower, beans, ladies finger, tomato, and other tubers like carrot, potato, radish etc are cultivated.

2.4 Physical Feature, Ornaments and Dress

The female's primary dress is called 'Chelakett'. It is a coloured material of 5-meter long cloth, like a sari. This is worn by folding over the body, just underneath the armpits, covering the bosom completely and tying the two ends of it over the left shoulder. They endeavour to keep the garments as conveniently and clean as could reasonably be expected. Youthful and educated young ladies like to wear skirts and shirts or pullovers and sari. Male dresses are shirts or banyan and Lungi or Mundu. Normally they don't have other types of garments to wear at formal events. Also, they don't have any traditional warm clothes either. The current generation of the Adiya tribe is interested in clothes made out of different materials like cotton, wool, silks, polyesters, types of denim etc. Female youngsters normally wear Churidars, Kurtis, Saree, Anarkali, Jeans and Pattu Pavada etc. Modern generation males prefer to wear Trousers, Cargo pants, Jeans, T-Shirts and Jerseys etc. Weather-based clothing style also had reflected among the dressing style of the current Adiya generation. Traditional clothes like Chelakett and Lungi/Mundu are these days worn only for ritual and other traditional ceremonies. Ornaments like Mookubettu (nose stud), Kathala (ear stud) and Kadagam (bangles) are usually worn by the female Adiya members despite different age groups.

2.5 Language

The language of the Adiya tribe is known as Ravula Bhasha, and they call themselves Ravular (endoname). Ravula language is a mixture of Malayalam, Tamil and Kannada languages, it resembles the language of the Yerava tribe of Karnataka. Ravula language belongs to the Dravidian language group, and it does not have a script. But now the tribal language is confined only to the colonies. They speak Ravula bhasha inside the house, and with other Adiya people only. Almost all of them are bilingual in nature and can speak Malayalam fluently. Adiya people converted to protestant Christianity were provided with the Ravula version of the Bible by using Malayalam script and this is the only existing written evidence of the Ravula language.

Table 2.1. Words in Ravula and its Translations in Malayalam & English

Ravula	Malayalam	English
Balli	Nellu	Paddy
Kaani	Illa	No
Thodakka	Thodakkam	Beginning
Kundalpani	Karar thoyilali	Bonded labour
Bally	Kooli	Wage
Anacharam	Anacharam	An uncivil act
Jammi	Janmi	Landlord
Kuntu	Cheari	Hamlet
Mookubettu	Mookuthi	Nose Stud
Kadagam	Vala	Bangle

2.6 Food Habits

The staple food of Adiya is rice. Ragi, Tubers, and other wild vegetables and leaves were a major food source in the olden days. Agricultural influence and bonded labour made the shift from the olden day's food menu to rice oriented menus. Also, as the returns for any work were paid in kind (paddy), they have to meet everyday necessities from it. They use rice with the least conceivable husking which was finished by hand. So there was very little loss of nutrients from husk expulsion. But nowadays the payments are paid in real money and they need to turn to a reasonable value to shop for rice. Attributable to the absence of work and cash, they need to forego frequently their weekly purchases. Some vegetables and green leaves are taken as subsistence. Adiya is essentially non-veggie lovers, however, beef-eating is forbidden at home. They eat chicken and other meats other than beef. Fish is smoked first and after that dried in the sun and put away in holder bushels. There are many myths related to their food habits. Few Adiya people are still facing sickle cell anaemia and few believe that they got this kind of disease only because their ancestors ate a lot of Crabs and Clams. Betel leaves and nuts find a place in every custom and ritual of Adiya people. They not only chew it with tobacco and slaked lime, but also use betel leaves and nuts as a cultural material to perform traditional activities and offerings. Without gender and age limits betel leaves and nuts are consumed at different times of the day. Kitchen gardening these days is promoted by Kudumbashree self-helping groups in every household. These kitchen gardens are producing different varieties of vegetables like brinjal, ladies finger, beans, tomatoes, cabbage and cauliflower etc for individual household consumption. Once a week, most Adiya households cook fish or chicken as a part of lunch or dinner. Other days mostly rice is taken with vegetables three times as cooked rice meal or as rice gruel (kanji) or rarely rice/wheat cuisines like dosha, chapati, puttu and appam for breakfast. Tubers are also cooked for any time, even evening snacks. But mostly the Adiya tribe eats rice as they were getting paid as paddy in the olden days and nowadays the government PDS (public distribution system) provides 20kg of rice per month for a household. The current generation prefers packed snacks and instant cooking food for evening snacks or occasional food. Many nutritious foods are provided by government schemes in colonies and schools.

2.7 Family Structure and Clans

The clan is the focal point of the social organization of a tribe, and the basic unit of each clan is the family. For the clan, they use the word 'Chemmam', and it is passed through the mother, each child of the family belongs to the mother's chemmam. Adiya people have a habit of living as joint and extended families but now because of the government schemes, Indira Awaas Yojana (IAY) majority of them shifted to a nuclear family system for better facilities. Father or Elder male is treated as the head of the family, both males and females in the family are earning members. Females get job opportunities through the MGNREGA (National Rural Employment Guarantee Act, 2005) scheme. Because of this females become more active in the decision-making process of the family. In a few families, males are addicted to alcohol where females act as the head and final decision-maker. Each family leads a peaceful and independent life. For them it is not compulsory to go separately after marriage both females and males can stay in their family after marriage according to their wish. Different clans in these three Adiya colonies are Momatte, Lakkot Mantu, Pudhari, Mantikya, Mantileru, Kachilakara, Mantile, Kalaikottu, Avilakaithy, Vadakku Mantu, Nattala, Kachikyan, Nalapady, Kachala and Evila. Adiya tribes are exogamous in nature, but if somebody wants to marry from his/her clan they have to pay a penalty to the Chemmakkaran, Kuntu moopan and Nattu Moopan.

2.8 Marriage Systems

Adiya marries from their community only. A young lady in puberty is viewed as qualified for marriage. The Thali(nuptial thread) and Toe-ring tell whether a female is married or not. Wedding rituals and celebrations happen at the bride's home that goes on for over one day. Each man should pay a sort of payment known as Thalappattom to the Chemmakkaran(clan head) either in real money or as a paddy, which is used for the organization of the clan. Marumakkathayam(matriliny) is followed among them. Adiya is exogamous and marries from different Chemmam only. If the distance between the bride's home and groom's home is far, then they can marry from the same Chemmam but different mantu and have to pay some fine. They don't have any customs of matching the horoscopes of people. Adiya doesn't have a horoscope recording system. Marrying from outside communities (non-adiyan tribes) is allowed these days. But there are some fine and rituals for that particular marriage to happen.

'Kanyala' means Marriage in the Ravula language. Marriage through negotiation starts first with the boy's father, mother's brother, and elder sister's husband visit the girl's house first. Then only if they agreed to the proposal boy and other close relatives go to visit the girl's house. Boy, carry gifts to a girl and her family at the time of visit, gifts like spices, paddy, betel leaves and nuts, vegetables and firewood etc. Nowadays boys are discussing their love affairs with elders in the community, to get blessings and helps from them for arranging official marriages. In such cases, Nattumoopan and the boy's father discuss the same with the girl's family and Nattumoopan of that Clan/Hamlet. Nattumoopan have a big role in conducting wedding fixation and ceremonies. Nattumoopan and his assistants will get certain payment for wedding ceremonies. Marriage ceremonies start at night time. The entire functions of marriage will last for a few days in different locations.

2.9 Kinship System

Kinship terminology of Adiya people is descriptive in nature, they are having their kin terms to address each kin and they are following it till now.

Table 2.2. Kinship Terms

Relationship	Kin Term
Father	*Appan*
Mother	*Awwa*
Elder brother	*Annan*
Elder sister	*Akki*
Younger brother	*Elavan*
Younger sister	*Thanga*
Grandfather	*Achappan*
Grandmother	*Ithiyamma*
Uncle (mother's brother)	*Maaman*
Aunty (mother's brother's wife)	*Maami*
Father's elder brother	*Perappan*
Father's elder brother's wife	*Peramma*
Father's younger brother	*Kooliyappan*
Father's younger brother's wife	*Kooliyamma*

Even though the Adiya tribe follow a matrilineal system, but they are giving more importance to patrilineal kins like any other non-tribal population in the colony. The responsibilities of patrilineal kins are more pronounced when compared to matrilineal kins.

2.10 Occupation and Economic Organization

Sex-based division of labour exists among the Adiya tribe. Men used to do heavy work like ploughing, taking loads, protecting agriculture fields from wild animals etc. Women used to do household works, cattle and kitchen garden caring, transplanting of paddy seedlings, composting and different plantation harvesting. Males are used to going out and far from home for any activities, this had reflected on the division of labour based on sex. Like heavy, distant, and fast works are taken by the male members while slow, easy, and nearby works are preferred by the female members of Adiya tribe. Both men and women are these days collecting firewood and other forest products for daily consumption. Firewood is collected on the way of returning home from the workplace or agriculture land. Adiya people are these days working as agricultural labourers, daily wage workers, household jobs, National Rural Employment Guarantee Activities (MGNREGA), Government schemes and Temporary works etc. Cattle rearing is another major economic source for daily life.

In the Bonded Labor System until the 1950-the 70s, Adiya were the main workers accessible in the region. For every 2.5 acres of land of paddy field, the landlords used to enlist one family unit of Adiya. Landowners attempt to pledge better talented and healthy Adiya families by paying in advance. During the 1950's advances of rupees, 25-50 were offered to Adiya families for a period of one year. Change of landlords results in the moving of residence to their landlords' territory. The reestablishing of bond or joining as a newcomer under another landlord and getting advances were made on the yearly celebration day of Valliyoorkavu Bhagavathy Temple. Adiya unequivocally has confidence in their diety's ability to punish for infringement of pledges. The daily payments to the Adiya family were paid in kind (paddy) i.e. 1 ½ seer for males and 1 seer for females (I seer = 1.25kg) in the evening. This paddy is husked using pestle and mortar, then extracted rice to cook food for the day. On special festival events like Onam and Vishu Adiya families are given one week's free payments (paddy), a few spices and new dresses for male individuals. A landowner would give one week's payment to a couple when an infant is born. The division of work as per sex is obvious. Males were required to furrow the land using bullocks, get ready farms, carry head loads, cut wood and protect crops from wild animals.

The females do replanting, segregating, manuring and gathering. The kids help to intend dairy cattle. After the yearly collection, the bonded workers were eligible to get a sort of reward called 'Kundal'. A family gets

250 seers of paddy. Throughout this time the advance payment (kind) was given to them before all else was produced against the 'Kundal'. When the family had cleared the overdue debts and got the remainder of the Kundal the family was free from the obligation of bonds. But normally no Adiya family could pay back all advances taken. In this manner, the entire family would remain attached to an existing landlord for quite a long time. The Adiya did not break this tie by going far or by different methods as they feared the power of the Valliyoorkavu Bhagavathy in whose name the exchange of advance and pledges were made.

2.11 Religion, Rituals and Customs

Adiya people worship lord Vishnu, lord Siva and Mariamman as their traditional goddess. According to their tradition, each clan is having their gods, but the name of that god will be different names of Shiva and Vishnu, i.e. ultimately they worship two gods, only their names are different. Nattumoopan is the supreme authority in their religion, he plays the role of Judge, Mediator, and Priest in their rituals and ceremonies. The religion of Adiya people never restricts them or compels them to worship and follow their traditional religion. They have their freedom to select their religion. But the people who select other religions are not allowed to participate in the rituals and ceremonies.

By the influence of Christian missionaries, some of them are converted to Protestants. There is one church in the Varinilam colony for converted Adiya people. Almost 10 families of the Varinilam colony converted to Christianity, but in official records, they belong to the Hindu religion, and they call themselves Hindus. Converted Adiya people are not allowed to participate in the rituals and ceremonies of Adiya people.

LIFE CYCLE RITUALS

Many life-cycle rituals (samskara) have been seen in most of the societies in the world. These ceremonies are performed during the special occasions of an individual like pregnancy period, birth, naming of the child, puberty ritual, marriage and death etc. every life cycle ritual has its own cultural and spiritual significance in each society. Major life cycle ceremonies of the Adiya tribe are Payattu, Irupathettu, Manjal Neer Kalyanam, birth and death rituals.

Peyattu: Peyyattu is the ritual that is performed at the 8th month of pregnancy to make a girl happy and to save her from evils. During pregnancy, all evils will try to attack the pregnant lady. To do this ritual people dress as devils, and sing and dance around the pregnant women. They try their level best to make her happy through their movements. Then they bring her to the Palm tree (according to their beliefs devils live in a Palm tree) to send all devils to the tree and return to the house without looking back. The ritual will end with a feast provided in the pregnant woman's house.

Birth Ceremony: when the lady gets labour pain she is confined to a room and seeks the help of Bethikarathi (midwife), who helps the mother in childbirth. She applies a paste of some medicinal plants into the pregnant lady's body to reduce the pain during delivery. The midwife cut the umbilical cord with a knife, and she took care of the infant and mother until the 28th day, only after the ritual Irupathettu she left the house. After childbirth, they make a bow and arrow with bamboo if a male child is born, and cradle it for the female child, then it is placed in front of the house to inform others about the gender of the newborn.

Irupathettu: Irupathettu is a ceremony that is performed on the 28th day after delivery to protect the baby from the evil eye by tieing a black thread on the infant's waist. This ritual is done in the father's house with all colony members and close relatives attending. Relatives will give gifts to the child during this ritual. Nattumoopan will tie a black thread to the child. Adiya people are not having any separate ritual for naming the child. Some of them do this with Irupathettu others can do it separately also. The name of the child is given by the Nattumoopan, by pronouncing the name in the child's ear three times. Usually, male children will be named with the grand father's name and female child with grand mother's name. Now they are not following it and giving modern names for their children is common. This ritual ends with a feast. Now they are doing this ceremony in a temple with close relatives, and the priest of the temple will take the nattu moopen's place.

Manjal Neer Kalyanam: Puberty ceremony of Adiya people is known as Manjal Neer Kalyanam. Manjal means Turmeric, Neer means water and Kalyanam means marriage. It is done on the 7th day of first menstruation, known as Vayasariyikkal among Adiya people. For seven days the girl is in pollution and is not allowed to go outside the house and light the traditional lamp called Vilakk. Only after the purification ceremony she can go out and light their traditional lamp. As the name suggests, during this ritual a girl will take bath in Turmeric water with the help of the father's elder or younger sister. According to their tradition, a girl will become a Ravula female only after this ritual. Girls have to wear the traditional dress of Adiya people (chelakkett). Dance and song will start only after the arrival of Nattumoopan, who officiates the ritual. The song of Manjal Neer Kalyanam is known as Sopanapattu. Everyone who comes for the ritual will give gifts to the girl, usually, the gifts will be dresses or ornaments for the girl. It will end with a feast provided in the house. Traditionally they serve vegetarian food but now they are giving non-vegetarian foods like chicken biryani.

Death Ritual: Adiya tribe are having three death rituals and all these rituals are done by Nattumoopan. After death, they give baths to the dead body in hot water with the help of Karimi (the person who assists Nattumoopan to do death rituals). After the death of a male person, they shave the moustache and beard of the dead body and dress up new. If it is female she will be dressed up as a traditional Ravula female with Chelakett and traditional ornaments. Nattumoopan will recite things that happened from a dead person's life (birth to death) and he will start Puja. Then Karimmi will make Manja(bamboo or wood cot) carry the dead body and will ask permission of each member of the family. Then Nattumoopan and assistants will take the dead body in Manja to a traditional cemetery. Before entering the cemetery Karimmi will ask permission of ancestors in the cemetery. With help of all the relatives, they pay the debts of the dead person and bury the dead body.

The next ritual is done on the second day of death in the house of the dead person. This ritual is known as Mudikalachil and this ritual is not done on Friday and Saturday, rather they wait for Sunday. Brothers and sons of dead people shave their heads in the presence of Nattumoopan during this ritual. Only male members are allowed to participate in this.

The last ritual of death is done on the 13th day of death. Nattumoopan with the help of other elders of the colony performed this ritual. He invokes Chudala Bhadrakali; the goddess of the cemetery, to help capture the soul of the dead in a bangle known as Peyy Vala. Peyy means ghost and Vala means bangle. And he covers the bangle with the one-piece cloth, for females they use saree and thorth (towel) for male. They will keep this for one year and release the soul after 1 year with a song transferring the soul to a temple in Kakkoor, Kozhikode district.

Kootta: During the month of March every year they celebrate Kootta for the remembrance of dead Adiya people. Kootta is a three-day ceremony where for two days they do Puja for their ancestors. The last day of Kootta is special, every youngster of the community are allowed to sing and dance on that day. They can mock everyone including the Nattumoopan. The dance done on this third day is known as Koottattu, for this, they make a temporary shed in the colony. Each colony performs a separate Kootta ceremony.

Traditionally they have the habit of chewing betel leaves and areca nuts with slaked lime, they offer this to people who come to their house as a mark of respect. The habit of chewing this is related to one mythical story. Itti and Achan (ancestors of the Adiya tribe) went to Pakkam to save themself from Mariamma. They reached the house of Pakkathappan (Vishnu) and pleaded with him to save them. When Mariamma came to Pakkam in search of Itti and Achan, Pakkathappan told her to sit under the shade of a jack fruit tree and he gave her betel leaf, a shell from the stream for slaked lime, and betel nut from the forest to her. When she started chewing this he also joined her. From then onwards Adiya people started using this. Tobacco was not culturally allowed but because of acculturation now they are using tobacco also.

According to Adiya tradition, all females and males needed to get a tattoo. They believed that doing tattoos will help them to reduce body pain. Females have to tattoo on their face and males in their hand. They use some medicinal plants and thorn of a plant to do tattooing. But now they are not practising this custom.

2.12 Traditional Art Forms

Adiya tribe have a rich cultural heritage among tribes of Kerala. They have an informal education system to transfer knowledge of art form to the next generation. The traditional knowledge about their art, dance, and crafts are transferred through male members of the tribe, and all these are performed by males only. Nattumoopan is the supreme authority who controls and has knowledge of all the art forms of Adiya.

Gadhika: Gadhika is one of the important dance forms of the Adiya tribe, Which is still having social acceptance. There are three types of Gadhika. 1) Cheriya Gadhika (Gadhika for curing disease), 2) Pooja Gadhika (If the disease is cured to express their happiness), and 3) Naduneekal or Nattu Gadhika (Gadhika for the protection of village). Gadhika is performed by the male members of the tribe. They have informal education for the male children to learn about this dance form and the person who performs Gadhika is known as Thammadi.

Cheriya Gadhika: When a person becomes ill his relatives will inform Nattumoopan that they wish to perform Gadhika for the ill person. The Nattumoopan will discuss with Thammadi the date and time that he can perform Gadhika. This Gadhika is performed in the house of the patient in the presence of relatives and colony members. Only Adiya people can participate on this occasion. This can be performed by one or more than one Thammadi together. The patient will sit on the veranda of the house, and dance will take place in the courtyard around a traditional lamp called 'Vilakku' with the sounds of their traditional instruments Thudi and Cheeni. Thammadi will sing-song while dancing, Nattumoopan also joins them in singing. There is no separate attire and makeup for doing this Gadhika. The Thammadi cover his head with a white towel called Thorth. During the dance, he will break the coconut and the family members of the patient will slice the coconut kernel into pieces to give everyone in the house, which is considered to carry the blessings of Mariamma. While dancing Mariamma will enter the Thammadi and he will go into trance and will bless the patient to regain his health quickly.

Pooja Gadhika: Puja Gadhika is performed when the person recovers from ill health, the patient's family inform the Nattumoopan that he is cured, to express this happiness and thanks to Mariamma by performing the Gadhika once again. Puja Gadhika can be performed in the house of Nattumoopan, Thammadi or the patient who recovered, according to the wish of Nattumoopan. They decide where the Gadhika should perform, for Puja Gadhika also performed like Cheriya Gadhika.

Naadu Neekal or Nattu Gadhika: This Gadhika is performed once a year for the protection of their village. Neighbouring colonies also do this performance together and it will last for 3 to 7 days. To do Nattu Gadhika, Thammadi has to go fasting for seven days. During these days he is not allowed to touch females because from the first day of fasting he will be considered as female. On the seventh day, before starting Gadhika, Thammadi has to take bath in the stream near Mariamman, and he goes to the Mariamman temple. Nattumoopan, Kuntumoopan of each colony, Chemmakkaran of each clan should participate in the puja at Mariamman temple with Thammadi. At the end of the puja, they take blessings from Parvathy (mother of Mariamma), Sivan (father of Mariamma), and Mariamman for the success of Nadu Neekal. First Thammadi performs Gadhika in Mariamman temple and Nattumoopan sang the Gadhika Pattu (Gadhika song). Then he moves to every house in the colony. Without considering the religious status of the household the Gadhika is performed in every house. During the time of the bonded labour system, Adiya is not permitted to enter into the landlord's house, but while performing nattu Gadhika they can enter into the landlord's house without any restriction. People will welcome the Thammadi into their house, and provide paddy, flowers, coconut and vilakku in their courtyard to perform Gadhika. Gadhika has an important role in keeping solidarity not only among the Adiya people but also in the whole village.

Dressing Style of Gadhika: Thammadi has to wear a red or rose colour silk saree, mani on his ankle (traditional anklet), bangles, maala (traditional necklace), hair extension and makeup like a female. Traditional materials used for makeup during

Nattu Gadhika is Kumkuma for Red, Turmeric for Yellow, Charcoal for Black, and Bhasma for white.

The myth of Gadhika: Adiya people relate Gadhika with the beginning of their life in Thrissilery. The mythical story behind Gadhika is related to the father and mother of Mariamma that is Siva and Parvathy. Before they worshipped both Siva and Parvathy at Thrissilery Mahadeva temple, during that time Parvathy's father arranged one puja (yaagam) in his place (according to their belief yaagam was conducted at Kottiyoor, Kannur, Kerala) but Siva and Parvathy are not invited for the puja. Parvathy wanted to attend the puja. Siva didn't restrict her but he told her that if she wouldn't get any respect, then he would not allow her to come back to Thrissilery. Parvathy didn't get any respect at Kottiyoor because of that Siva became angry and he sent his devils to destroy Kottiyoor. After destroying the entire Kottiyoor Siva's devil started to disturb the Adiya people of Thrissilery. Adiya people asked Mariamma to protect themselves from Siva's devils. Mariamma helped Adiya people by capturing all devils with her cane. In the remembrance of this Adiya people started to celebrate Gadhika. They believe that each year after the festival in Kottiyoor temple devils from Kottiyoor will come and disturb people in Thrissilery, to save the village from these devils Thammadi will perform Gadhika. According to them while performing Gadhika Thammadi possesses Mariamma. They also believed that the disease is because of devils, that's why they started to do Gadhika to cure the disease.

Kambara Nirtham: It is a dance performed by Adiya people during the collection of new saplings from the paddy field. Women collect paddy saplings from the nursery and men sing and dance around the field with their traditional instruments Thudi and Cheeni. Women wear usual working clothes and male performers wear red shawl on the head in traditional ways. They sing and move around the paddy fields while the ladies gather new saplings from the field. Kambara Nritham is Adiya communities dance to express their respect towards agriculture practices.

Kootattu: Kootattu is a dance form performed by the youngsters of the community on the third day of the Koota ritual. Kootattu doesn't have special or uniform dance moves. Anybody can dance according to their wish along with the group. Kootta rituals act as a platform to get together with all members of the community or colony.

Vellattu Dance: The dance done along with the Vellattu ritual is known as the Vellattu dance. Thammadi of the colony performed this dance. He has to wear white dhoti on his waist while doing this dance.

Traditional Songs: Adiya has several traditional songs about different life/cycle events. Sopanapattu for Manjal neer kalyanam (puberty ceremony), Pulapattu, Leelalapattu for Koota (death ritual), Poiganapattu for Marriages, and Chembanapattu for worshipping Mariamma. These are some traditional songs of the Adiya tribe, which are followed tradition only during related ceremonies. But the current generation is not interested in learning these songs.

Traditional Instruments: Thudi: It is a percussion instrument made of wood of Jackfruit tree and goatskin. This traditional instrument is used in all life cycle rituals of the Adiya tribe i.e. death ritual, puberty ceremony, marriage, pregnancy ritual etc.. and also in traditional dances. Cheeni: Cheeni is also made up of the wood of the Jackfruit tree and Coconut shell. It is a flute-like instrument used along with Thudi.

2.13 Political Organizations

Adiya tribes of Wayanad district are divided into three geographical areas and it is again classified into colonies, colony is divided as phratries and phratry is divided as clans.

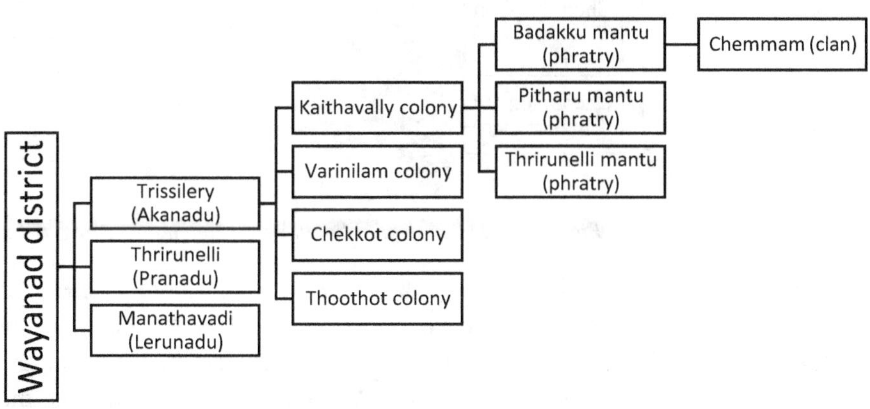

Figure 1. The political organization of Adiya tribe communities.

Figure 1 shows that the geographical area of Thrissilery is divided into four colonies that are Kaithavally, Varinilam, Chekkot and Thoothot. Phatry classification is the same for all colonies, for them, it is compulsory to include all three phratries in each tribal colony and they call phratry as Mantu the decisions of Mantu is taken by the elders of the Mantu along with the Nattumoopan and Kuntumoopan. The hierarchy of political power is described in figure 2 Nattumoopan is the supreme authority of the village and the final decision is taken by him. Kuntumoopan is the chief of the tribal colony and he enjoys the decision of higher political status in his colony. Mantu elders have the power to take the decisions inside the Mantu and Chemmakaran have the power to decide on the clan. Problems of the lower levels are solved by concerned chiefs, the problem that can't be solved by them will go for higher levels for a solution and the ultimate decision is taken by the Nattumoopan.

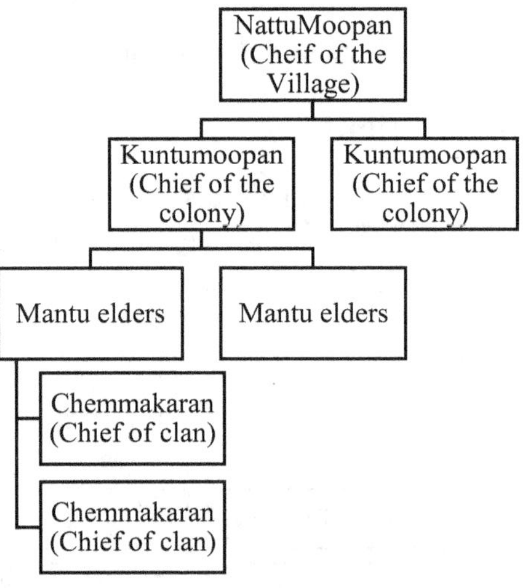

Figure 2. Hierarchy of political power among the Adiya tribe.

Selection of Nattumoopan is done by the elders of the village, there is no age limit to become Nattumoopan, any one of the tribe can become the Nattumoopan but he has to learn about all the rituals, ceremonies, songs, art forms and myths related to Adiya tribe. Village elders will examine the person, he has done all the rituals, performs all dance forms and say all the myths to the elders then only they will allow him to become Nattumoopan and he can enjoy the position lifelong. Nattumoopan can only be changed according to the wish of the present Nattumoopan or by the death of him.

Thammadi who performs Gadhika is the assistant of Nattumoopan, he has to assist Nattumoopan in all religious and political occasions. All religious functions, rituals and ceremonies are controlled and done by the Nattumoopan. The selection of Kuntumoopan and Chemmakaran is done by the member of Kuntu (colony) and Chemmam (clan) respectively. Usually, the elder members of the unit will be selected as the respective head. Traditionally the village was controlled by the Nattumoopan. The traditional attire of Nattumoopan is a shirt and dhothi with a red shawl tied over his head. And he has to carry his stick every time. After democracy, his position confined to religious functions only. Now they are having a modern political organization also with a traditional political organization. Nowadays, few chiefs have also contested in panchayath elections. One of the chief from this area have worked as a ward member during 2005-2010.

32

ETHNOGRAPHIC PROFILE OF ADIYA TRIBE, KERALA

3
MODERNIZATION

Modernity has a deep establishment in overall casings for conceptualizing the Economical, Socio-Cultural, Political and Emotional changes that emerged with the result of colonization and globalization. Modernity refers to the change in different levels of individual or community or a whole country at various spheres as pointed out. Changes are reflected in internal and external aspects of institutions like Religion, Marriage, Kinship, Occupation, Political organization, Health etc. Change brings deviations from traditional systems and that is considered modernisation. Modernisation factors are impacted by Tribal populations with various aspects of life. A large number of examples were offered to show that a tribe was never completely isolated. It entered into a set of relationships with its neighbouring communities, tribals as well as non-tribals (Bose 1971: 4; Dube 1977: 2). Tribal communities were always struggling to cope up with their social and natural conditions to ensure their continuity. They were most neglected over the decades. The development of the tribal population had emerged from different institutions with the impact of modernisation and other allied forces. In India, many tribal movements had happened in different locations to protect and ensure growth. Kerala had showcased several movements for land rights, employment guarantee and tribal women empowerment. These movements resulted in governments introducing many schemes to empower tribal peoples as self -sufficient communities. Organisations like Kudumbashree, Government's programmes, NGOs, and local tribal organisations along with external tangible and intangible influences of Globalisation, Industrialisation and Modernisation played a good role to bring the Adiya community to modernity. The concept of modernisation in tribal hamlets starts from a change in thoughts, viewpoints and lifestyles that have a direct connection with socio-cultural and economic aspects of tribal identity and community. Impact of modernisation happened on Ideological level, Technological level, and Basic Amenities and Facilities etc.

Modernity or Modernisation is the result of changes taking place in different aspects. Some are tangible and others are intangible changes. One generation's change was modern in that social time and space, later the same change became tradition/olden to another generation. For every time and space, the change has two directions, way back and way forward. Thus the concept of modernity exists in every era/time of society. Where some are at an ideological level and others are technological levels of changes.

3.1 Ideological Level

An ideological level change reflects in the way of thinking, thoughts, viewpoints, attitude and behavioural expressions etc. First ideological change happens then it brings the social changes in society. The Adiya tribe also exhibited changes in traditional practices, belief systems and customs. According to the Nattumoopan (Karian) of Thrisillery village, 'Agricultural practices had a lot of rituals in olden times. Adiya had the tradition of just scattering seeds in a small part of the field before starting agriculture for the year. They wait for some time without watering or manuring the field. If the seeds are grown without caring they cultivate larger areas in that season otherwise they won't'. This belief of considering goddesses to have all the power to grow agriculture is less these days and this custom is not existing in the current generation. Now they have faith in good quality seeds, proper watering, and scientific fertilizing that provide good agricultural results. As Adiya are agricultural experts from the olden days, their traditional point of view had changed, the journey towards modernity had established a few years back itself. Likewise, thoughts on different aspects of life had changed. Belief systems, Health, Economy, Education, Lifestyle, Political system and Language etc had been impacted by the process of Modernization.

Belief Systems: Belief system, Customs, Rituals and Myths are slowly forgotten by the current generation of Adiya. Traditional customs related to agriculture, marriage, death ceremony, puberty celebration, Art forms and Religion etc are not fully followed and also traditions have changed with the influence of modernisation factors. Pure traditional rituals or customs are altered as that favour modern social conditions and followed by the current generation only on very special occasions. Adiya communities are constantly interacting with the political ideology of communism from the pre-independence period itself. This also made a change in most of their religious viewpoint. It has reflected that many Adiya leaders were ardent followers of communist ideologies and not promoted/inherited any religious ideologies among the last few generations. Cross-cultural interaction made them trust and accept all kinds of religious people around them. There are a few converted family cases in Thrissilery village itself. From the older generation Adiya believed in gods like Shiva, Vishnu and supreme goddess Mariamma but now a few people have converted to Christianity. A converted Adiya family head describes the reason to choose Christianity as his disease was healed by Jesus. Also, another 70-year-old grandmother who is an expert in Ayurvedic fracture healing started to attend Holy Mass at the nearest church after her disease was cured by church sisters. Christianity was not there in olden times in Adiya habitats. Few are accepting Christianity as a modern religion to solve most of the existing problems faced. Same time there is a trend of Atheist ideologies among a few people as a result of communism ideologies. Changes happened in the marriage customs also. Love marriages have become very common. In the case of arranged marriage, the likes and dislikes of girls are also considered nowadays. Females are enquiring about the educational status and job of the man whom they are going to marry. The custom of bride price is not practised now, and dowry doesn't have any space in their marriage system. This reflects a change in traditional belief systems to accept modern ideologies and concepts of social lifestyles.

Social Life & Political System: Social life includes how people interact within a community and outside the community. Adiya of Thrissilery village is living in harmony with non-tribal communities like Muslims, Christians and Hindus, who migrated from south Kerala districts. The nearest shops in Kaithavally and Varinilam are owned by non-tribals and interaction between them is routine. This had brought Adiya the character of accommodations and adjustment. Earlier Adiya was afraid of outsiders. Even male members hide inside houses when outsiders come to the colony. Constant interaction with non-tribal people, education and other government agencies made Adiyas more social these days. Now Adiya accepts all cultural people with love and care. Political views also had changed a lot. Even they follow their traditional political system, the modern political system and its concept is well established. They were supporting many outside political parties to demolish the bonded labour system and British colonisations. The Left-wing of Kerala was supported by Adiya communities earlier. Now overall the Adiya community doesn't have any single political view. Most of them support the left-wing and a few other parties. Including the Moopan many Adiya were Jailed when fighting for their rights and needs. P.K. Kalan and C. K. Janu are notable political leaders from Adiya. The need for Democracy and other modern political systems are known by Adiya communities.

Economic System: Long back itself Adiyans had accepted and gained proper knowledge about cash transactions than the barter system. During the bonded labour system Adiya were getting wages in kind like Paddy and they used to exchange it for any other everyday items. Now things have changed along with changes happening in surrounding economic systems. They are getting wages as cash, spending the same for purchasing other goods and services. Other schemes, grants, and subsidies take place through bank transactions. This made everyone have bank accounts, youngsters are using online bank payments for different needs. The concept of money and the basic banking system are well understood by Adiya.

Healthcare and Education: Traditional medical system was there among Adiya for many centuries. But the current generation doesn't have any knowledge about traditional medicines. According to Moopan, the previous generation did not share any information regarding traditional medicinal knowledge with the current generation and he felt guilty about it. Modern Allopathic medicine is prefered by all Adiya people these days. Only a few common medicinal plants are used to cure diseases like fever, cold, and cough. The reason behind preferring modern medicine over traditional techniques is because traditional knowledge has been lost and modern medicine has become easily available with fast recovery effects. Governments and Christian missionaries have a major role in this health care ideological transformation. Government medical centres are providing Allopathic medicine and Asha workers to every ward in Thirunelli grama panchayath. Modern medicinal treatment methods and the concept of allopathic diseases curing systems are fully accepted by the Adiya people now. People in the Varinillam colony go to Kurichia shaman in the colony if the modern allopathic medicine fails, Kaithavally and Chekkot colony people prefer to go to Ayurveda hospital in Kattikulam (10 KM from Thrissilery) if allopathic medicine fails. One of the main reasons for this shift is that people lost faith in their traditional medicine and its knowledge. Now almost 98% of them like allopathic medicine more than traditional and ayurvedic medicine because it helps in quick healing. They are having a government health centre almost 1 KM far from the colony. The Asha worker from the health centre visits each house in the colony twice or thrice a week and will give the necessary medicines and health advice to them. Other than Asha workers each colony has a helper known as Oorumitra, who helps the Asha worker in her work and also carries the diseased person to the health centre. The Oorumitra of each colony belongs to the Adiya tribe. The major health problem faced by Adiya people in Thrissilery is Sickle Cell Anemia. As many as 4 Adiya children and one 26-year-old female having sickle cell anaemia in Varinilam and Kaithavally colony. They are getting special assistance from the Asha worker and Oorumitra. Sickle Cell Anemic person is getting 2000 rupees per month and also 3kg portions of cereal per month from the health centre.

While considering the sources of modernisation, formal education has an important role. Compulsory and free education up to the 10th standard and grants from the government helps Adiya children to go to school. Also, they are having a jeep for children up to 10th standard to go to school and also breakfast at school. Elders' viewpoint towards formal education had changed a lot. Nowadays they are trying to educate children maximum to get a better job. There is a public library near Kaithavally Colony which has a different new paper, Magazines, Novels and Computer browsing options with Xerox and Scanning services. Monthly library officers' conduct different types of competitions to encourage youngsters to spend time at the library. In 2019, a Kurichiya tribal girl from Wayanad had bagged 410th rank in the IAS exam. She was the first tribal girl to get IAS rank from Kerala. This will further motivate tribal kids to dream big. Attitude towards different types of technical education is changing these days.

Lifestyle, Nutrition & Hygiene: Overall views on lifestyle had changed. Adiya is consuming different kinds of meats, fruits, vegetables and packed foods to have good nutritious foods. The government is providing nutritious food to pregnant women, children, and aged people daily lunch in community kitchens. Pregnant women and infants are given special nutritious foods like Horlicks, Boost, PediaSure etc. Proper breastfeeding also practised from their traditional days itself. Special food menus are provided for people with chronic or inborn diseases. Hygiene is also maintained well at personal and community. Every household has a latrine outside, a few with tilted and European closets. They are using soaps, washing powders, and toilet clears to keep hygiene in their lifestyle.

3.2 Technological Level

Technological level changes include the change happening in technology and because of the technology. These days' technologies are changing faster than human behavioural adaptability. Even before the person fully attains or adapts to a certain technology, change happens for the same technology. The reason is technologies are rapidly updating when compared to humans adaptation to technologies. Today it is the world of the Internet of things and the innovations are reaching the hands of the common man's hand in a short time. India as a developing country and with the impact of Globalisation worldwide innovations are accepted and consumed in every corner. Adiya also moved further in technological advancements like any other rural societies. Gone those days where tribes are uneducated or depend only on indigenous techniques. They started to adopt modern technologies where their indigenous technologies did not fulfil their requirements. Here the technological level includes Information & Communication Technologies, Banking technology, Housing and Daily life amenities, Online/Digitalisation, Citizen digital identity records/registration etc.

Information and Communication: Overall India itself had witnessed a communication technology revolution after the introduction of 4G and Fiber networking cables. ICT includes Television, Internet, Mobile phones, Smart gadgets, DTH services and other modern communication apps and gadgets. As technologies became more feasible and available, Adiya tribals also started to adopt different information and communication technologies. Most of the households have mobile phones and Television. More than half of the households have a smartphone. The electricity had come to these areas 15-18 years back. The availability of electricity was there for different technological appliances. All the TVs are connected to any DTH (Direct to Home) service provider. TVs become part of their daily life routine. LCD, LED TVs are used by a few families. They brought costly TVs on Installment mode of payment. According to informants Entertainment is the major purpose of watching TV. The current generation watches other languages like Tamil, Hindi and Telugu TV Channels. English information and entertainment channels are followed by the younger generation. Radio was there in earlier days. But now TVs are becoming more popular. The recent trend is watching Television programmes on Smartphones. Internet usage in smartphones is common. Smartphones are used for Entertainment, Social networking and Multimedia Gaming. There are a few active users of the Chinese online video sharing app 'TIK TOK' which is very popular recently among youngsters. Whatsapp groups of different friendship circles, education updates, news updates and job updates are subscribed by the youngsters. This advancement in ICT has impacted positively and negatively like any other people. ICT ensures updated information sharing on things happening inside their community and outside in the world.

Housing and Technology: Before settling in the Wayanad Adiya tribe were in a nomadic lifestyle. Those days they had travelled from one place to another with few cattle to get resources to consume and sustain life. An earlier settlement in Wayanad was like a circular form where all houses were surrounded by a stone called 'Achan' in the ground. Now all this system had changed to modernised individual houses of small families. The government had provided free houses to most of the Adiya tribe families. This influenced each family to live separately in different houses in scattered locations. 95% of the Adiya households have an electricity connection. Also, modern amenities like TV, DTH, Mobile Phone, LPG,

Grinder Mixie and other Electronic gadgets are available. Few houses have Washing machines and refrigerators also.

Banking System and other Online Services: The Adiya people are knowledgeable about basic banking systems and concepts. The government had changed all monetary transactions like Grants, Scholarships, Salaries, Pensions, Schemes and Subsidies etc only through a bank account of the individual. This made the opening of bank accounts from school kids to old people. ATM technology is used by the younger generation. Few people use online banking for payment of different services and shopping sites. The concept of a cashless economic system is awarded by youngsters as well as elders. Another reason to open a bank account is to take Bank Loans for personal purposes like house renovation, marriage, disease treatments, agricultural equipment and education needs. Governments had influenced Adiya to understand and open bank accounts from some years before. Other than banking, online shopping and E-District services of Government are availed by the community. Flipkart and Naaptol are mostly prefered by users in Thrissilery village. Usually, they buy clothes, shoes and electronic gadgets which are not available in nearby places or costly in the town. Cash on delivery payment method is chosen normally. Kerala government is providing many services online where a citizen can avail services like Revenue department certificate services, Right To Information service, Public Grievance services, Different payment services, Revenue court cases and Forest department services. To ensure maximum utilisation of these services the government had established E-Seva Kendra in different rural areas. Thrissilery village has one E-Seva Kendra at Pallikavala.

Citizen Digital Identity Registrations and Voting: Registrations for Voter ID, Aadhaar, and Digital PDS are other technological advancements and challenges fully accepted by the Adiya tribe. 100% of Adiya in Thrissilery village are registered to Voter ID, Aadhar and PDS. They had faced difficulties to get registered but many local organisations and government local officers provided good support. Biometric information recording made many confused and fearful. But now Adiya is using Fingerprint to take PDS products and other Aadhaar linked services. The concept of digital registration is accepted and maximises its utilisations for services like opening bank accounts, government subsidies, school enrolments, SIM card registration, PDS, E-District sevas and PDS. Adiya also experienced both Ballot paper and Electronic Voting Machine systems. The introduction of EVMs confused but providing a proper demonstration of EVMs facilitated acceptability. For the 2019 Lok Sabha election, VVPAT (Voter-Verified paper Audit Trail) System is introduced in 543 Lok Sabha constituencies. The election commission gives proper information regarding VVPAT to all citizens including the Tribal settlements.

Table 3.1. Tradition to Modernity Transition Trends

	Traditional practice	**Current practice**
Housing	Charcoal and Cow Dung flooring.	Cemented and Tiled flooring.
	Paddy Straw, Coconut leaves, Wood and Bamboo Roofing.	Tiled, RCC, Corrugated roofing sheets.
	Firewood.	LPG & Induction Cooker.
	Radio.	TV & DTH.
	Open Toilet.	Closed and Tiled Toilets.
	Natural and Cloth Mops/Brooms.	Plastic & Fiber Mops/Brooms.
	Water in big Clay Pots.	Plastic Water Tanks and Plumbing systems.
	Cleaning with Neem leaves and charcoal ash.	Chemical cleaning agents like Harpic, Vim etc.
	Ammikallu (hand grindstones) and Ural (big granite pestle and mortar).	Electric Mixi Grinder and Wet Grinder
Food Habits	Vegetable Leaves and Tubers (Cassava, Sweet Potato, Elephant Foot Yam etc).	Rice, Wheat, etc (grain products).
	Local Fish, Crabs, Clams etc.	Chicken, Sea Fish, Meats (expect Beef).
	Betel nuts.	Packed Pans.
	Rice and Ragi malt soups.	Pediasure, Horlicks, Boosts etc.
	Local raw fruit/seed/tubers for snacks.	Multi Brand Packed Snacks, Sweets, Cookies etc.
	Local Fruits like Jackfruit, Cashew mango, Papaya etc.	Apple, Orange, Grapes and Pomegranate.
	Beef eating is taboo.	Beef eating taboo only at home.
Dressing Style	Male: Lungi/Mundu and Thorth(Towel).	Elders: Lungi and Shirts / T-shirts Youngsters: Jeans/Cargo pants and Shirts / T-shirts.

	Female: Chelakkett.	Elders: Maxi Dresses or Saree. Youngsters: Salwar, Churidaar, Kurta, Saree, Pattu Pavada and Jeans pants.
Daily Materials	Coconut fibre or Banana fibre Ropes.	Plastic Ropes.
	Charcoal ash powder or Tree leaves for brushing tooth.	Tooth Paste and Tooth Brush.
	Wooden and Clay Utensils.	Glass and Steel Utensils.
	Paddy Straw/Bamboo Mats.	Plastic Mats & Cotton Beds.
	Water washing.	Washing Powder, Soap, Shampoo, Dettols and other cleaning agents.
	Barefoot tradition.	Plastic Chappals and Shoes.
	Wooden comb.	Plastic Comb.
	Wooden & Clay pots.	Plastic bottles, Thermos & Flasks
Language	Ravula	Ravula, Malayalam, Tamil, Kannada and English
Games	Kuttiyumkolum, Pallanguzhi, Goli, Hide-n-Seek, Seven Stones.	Football, Carrom, Cricket, Badminton and Multiplayer smartphone games.
Education and Knowledge sharing	Only Informal education and Traditional knowledge sharing.	Modern School system, Tutions, Work oriented training and Higher education.
Marriage	Strictly Endogamous (tribe).	Relaxation in Endogamy.
	Vegetarian Food called Sadhya as reception food.	Biryani and other non-veg food menu prefered more.
Healthcare practice	Natural & Homemade Medicines and Medical treatments.	Fully depend on Allopathic medicine.

44

ETHNOGRAPHIC PROFILE OF ADIYA TRIBE, KERALA

4
ACCULTURATION

Acculturation is the process of social, cultural, and psychological change that stems from the balancing of two cultures, where one group adopts the culture of the other. Acculturation taking place in all multi-cultured societies around the world, and also in the indigenous communities. Tribal acculturation is social, cultural and psychological changes taking place in the life of a tribal group because of the influence of tribal development programs, formal education, non-tribe and other tribes, different facilities etc…A large number of examples were offered to show that a tribe was never completely isolated. It entered into a set of relations with its neighbouring communities, tribal as well as non-tribal (Bose 1971; Dube 1977). These interactions lead to too many changes in the lifestyle of these people. Tribal communities where lived a peaceful life in their habitat, but because of many reasons they forced to migrate to other places and now they are struggling to come up to mainstream society. They are working hard to get better social status because the tribal were considered inferior to other social groups because of their primitive technologies, backwardness and vulnerability etc. and they were exploited by the non-tribal groups. To overcome the exploitation and to get equal rights many tribal movements had happened all over India. Kerala also faced many tribal movements and because of these governments introduced many tribal development and empowerment programs for them, and it became another reason for the changes that happened to the life of the tribe.

The traditional practices of ethnomedicine, dressing style and ornaments and food habits are slowly disappearing from their culture, rituals, ceremonies, political and economic organization are mixed-up with modern practices. The younger generation of the tribe is unaware of their culture and traditional practices; they already changed to the modern way of life. Formal education plays an important role in the habits and lifestyle of youngsters of the community, and they influence the elders of the tribe. They are very familiar with the modern lifestyle because of the use of television, smartphones, social media networking sites etc.

Family Structure: Family is a group of people related either by consanguinity or affinity and shares the same residence. The no of members and the type of kins in the family makes different kinds of families such as nuclear family, extended family, joint family etc. All Adiya houses in the colony are provided by the government through the

Indira Awas Yojana (IAY) or Pradhan Mantri Gramin Awas Yojana (PMAY-G), a social welfare flagship programme created by the Indian government to provide housing for the rural poor in India. Benefits from the government become easily accessible from 2000 for the Adiya people because of their former tribal chief P K Kalan. It results in a tendency to make a new house for the elder couple of the family among Adiya people even though they already have a government allotted house. Slowly acculturation took place in their family structure through the government facilities and schemes.

Economic Exchanges: Acculturation in economic exchange take place in many ways, the major reason is the change of traditional occupation to a new one, even though 80% of them are still unskilled manual labours. The traditional occupation of them is agricultural works and they were under the bonded labour system during the 50-70s. Through the bonded labour abolition act in 1976, they become free from the forced labour, but they continued to work in the fields. A decrease in cultivation leads them to search for new jobs. Now they are going for other unskilled manual labourers like construction works, painting, cleaning etc... Females are going for the Mahatma Gandhi Rural Employment Guarantee scheme and other unskilled manual works like cleaning, household works etc. Some of them are ready to go to other districts in search of a better job to earn more money, that made them know about different people, culture, food habits etc... Such people returns only thrice or twice a year to their home. And it changed their way of living up to some extent. The average income of an Adiya man per day is 500 INR and for women, it is 350 INR. Few of them having government jobs or other government fellowships like the Gadhika training fellowship.

There is a shift from the traditional occupation to a new one. The main reason is the lack of agricultural works, and they can earn more money from other manual labours than agricultural work. It results in more acculturation in the food habits of the people especially the person who going to town for work.

Food Production and Food Habit: The food production and food habit of the Adiya people changed a lot during the past 20 years, and the major reason for the change is acculturation. The person who is going for work outside the colony (especially male) has a space to know and taste the outside food, and he will introduce the food item to the whole family. One example is that they are having beef now, according to the Adiya culture eating beef is taboo, but lack of religious ties and exposure to the outer world made them break the cultural taboo. Still some elders in the colony especially females won't eat beef and don't allow others to cook beef in house. Most of them will have beef from hotels and outside shops, but in some houses, they are cooking beef occasionally.

During that time of bounded labour, they used to cultivate paddy, banana, and other vegetables in the field, and they will get wage as paddy. But now they are not cultivating paddy and vegetables, only a few of them are having coffee cultivation. Almost 90% of the households are having a kitchen garden, but it is not enough for them. They already lost the sustainable kitchen garden that traditionally they had; now the new trend is started a few years back through Kudumbashree. Now they are cultivating beans, a local verity of spinach, chilly, cauliflower, cabbage, sweet potatoes etc. in their kitchen garden in grow bags. Acculturation took place in the way of producing vegetables in the kitchen garden. But still, they are using the traditional fertilizers for kitchen garden i.e. cow dung and urine of cow. Leafs had an important place in their meals, they used to cook leaves of different vegetables such as pumpkin, beans, different local verity tubers, bottle gourd and also local varieties of spinach, they call this as "chappu". But a decrease in the cultivation during the past 10 years reduced the availability of leaves, it affected their food habits. They forced to buy vegetables from the shop even though they have a kitchen garden, availability of small grocery shop locally made them easy to buy things. It introduced instant noodles (Maggi), readymade bread, cakes, cookies, nutrition drinks such as Horlicks, Boost, Pediasure etc. to their food habits. Only the elderly people in the colony knows about the edible leaves that they used to have before, the new generation is unaware of the edible leaves, and the traditional way of making food with these leaves.

The traditional way of cooking food is by firewood and they are following it till now. But acculturation took place in the way of cooking food through the government schemes that provided them LPG gas facility, and through instalment sellers. The way of grinding food items changed in past few years, mixer grinder replaced the traditional 'Ammikallu' (mortar). Traditionally they prefer to eat vegetarian food more but now they like to eat non-vegetarian food items more. Youngsters like biriyani and other fast foods more than homely food.

Table 4.1. Major changes related to food in Adiya tribal communities.

Traditional Practices	Current Practice	Reasons
More leaves in the food. Uses all edible leaves. Grow vegetables in the kitchen garden.	Fewer leaves. Don't know about all edible leaves. Purchase vegetables from the local shop.	Less cultivation. Very fewer vegetables in the kitchen garden.
Paddy from the field as wage. Separate rice from the husk in-home using 'ural' and 'ulakka' (mortar).	Money as a wage. Gets rice from government ration store.	The decrease in paddy cultivation.
Traditional grinding stones called 'Ammikallu' and 'ural' for grinding things.	Mixer grinder.	Availability of electricity. Availability of mixer grinder through instalment scheme. Easy to use.
Firewood for cooking food.	Using LPG stow and Induction cooker along with firewood.	Availability through the instalment scheme. A government scheme for providing LPG cylinder and stow.
Ragi and tubers (Cassava, Sweet Potato, Elephant Foot Yam etc) are the major food items.	Rice and Wheat become major food item. Tubers become only an evening snack.	A decrease in cultivation. Availability of rice through government ration shop.
Ragi and other traditional food were given to the children for growth.	Horlicks, Boost and PeadiaSure etc. Instant noodles, biscuits, cookies, Lays become the favourite food of children.	Availability of these items at an affordable rate (sample packs). Availability of these things in nearby shops Influence of advertisements.
Eating beef is taboo.	They started to eat beef from hotels, especially males. Some of them started cooking beef at home.	Influence of non-tribal people like Christians. Weak cultural ties.
Prefer very less non-vegetarian food.	Frequently eat fish and egg.	Availability of fish through mobile fish sellers. They are getting money as a wage. Availability of non-vegetarian food items

		in the nearby market.
Vegetarian meals in festivals and ceremonies.	Prefer biryani and other non-vegetarian food more.	Influence of other communities, hotels, restaurants.

Rituals, Customs and Religious Beliefs: Like the acculturation in other faces of life, religion also went through acculturation. They belong to the Hindu religion and worship Vishnu and Siva as their gods. Every lineage is having its god, but the name of the god will be a different name of Vishnu and Siva. Other than Vishnu and Siva they worship Mariamma as their traditional god because she saved their village from Siva's anger. But religious ties are very weak among them now. They are not willing to go to Mariamma's temple, only during nattu Gadhika they will go and worship Mariamma. Now they are going to the Trissileri Mahadeva temple (temple of non-tribal people) and participating in the rituals and ceremonies of the temple. Acculturation reflects in the rituals and ceremonies. The influence of non-tribal people, television, and market availability is the main reason for this.

Manjal Neer Kalyanam: puberty ritual of Adiya tribe is known as Manjal Neer Kalyanam. Many changes happened to this ritual because of the influence of the non-tribal population. Now they are serving non-vegetarian food instead of traditional vegetarian meals and they are not using traditional chelakett during this ritual as they prefer to wear modern dresses.

Marriage: Marriage ceremony is very important among them, but many changes happened to the marriage ceremony in the past 15 years. Cheakket the traditional way of wearing a saree was compulsory for the bride during the marriage, but now most of them prefer to wear a saree as the non-tribal people used to wear. The food given in the marriage ceremony was vegetarian, but now they like to give non-vegetarian foods like biriyani. Giving a bride price was compulsory in their culture, if somebody marries without giving the bride price means he has to pay a penalty. But now marriage without bride price and dowry is very common and no one is giving the penalty. Traditionally marriage is done in the bride's house, but now they are doing marriage in temple-like other non-tribes.

Peyyatu: Peyyattu is the ritual performed at the eighth month of pregnancy to save the pregnant lady from evils. During this ritual, people will dress as devils and sing and dance around pregnant women and make them happy. But now the ritual Peyyattu is performed very rarely, if it is performed only dance and song will be done.

Irupathiettu: The ritual performed after birth on 28th day to tie waist chain especially black thread on the waist of the child to save him/her from evils. Still, now they are performing this ritual, but traditionally the ritual is done in the house by the Nattumoopan but now they are doing it in the temple and the Nattumoopan's place is replaced by a priest of the temple. This change is happened because of the influence of the non-tribal population, because non-tribal people celebrate Irupathiettu, in the temple.

Funeral: the funeral is the only ritual that still performed traditionally, Nattumoopan is the important person and he leads the funeral ritual.

Gadhika: Gadhika is the dance form of the Adiya tribe that still they follow because it gives economic benefits to some of them through the government. Only nattu Gadhika is performed now, Gadhika for curing disease is not done commonly because they do not believe in Gadhika that it will cure disease. Traditionally while performing Gadhika to cure the disease they used to give ethnomedicine to the sick person but the practice of giving medicine they lost and also the belief in Gadhika.

These are some changes that happened in the life cycle rituals and religious practices of the Adiya people. Another important change that happened in their religion is through the influence of Christian missionaries. The influence of Christian missionaries is more in the Varinilam colony because there is a tribal mission church near to that colony. The church is for Christian converted tribes not for other Christians. About 10 tribal families of the Varinilam colony is converted to protestant. They converted to Christianity to overcome problems like alcoholism, disease etc. They call themself Hindus but beliefs in Jesus Christ. The trend of conversion started 15 years, and they are not allowed to participate in the rituals of the Adiya people. The rituals and ceremonies of converted Adiya families will be managed by the priest along with the prayer. The rate of conversion is increasing know because the church is helping the people to get a good education, overcome alcoholism, and also giving allopathic medicines to them.

To convert to protestant they have to take bath in the pond near the church and believe in Jesus, it is the baptism ritual for them (only adults). Like

Gadhika the converted people will perform prayer in the house of diseased person with a priest, they will also do fasting to cure disease, and also collect money to give the diseased person. Like Adiya people the converted Adiya also do Irupathettu, manjal neer kalyanam and peyyattu but instead of puja they will do prayer, and instead of Nattumoopan, the priest will do the ritual. There is a Sunday school for the converted people's children to learn about Christianity and Jesus, 20 children from 10 converted families are going to Sunday school. There is no traditional restriction in the Adiya community against conversion, but converted people are not allowed to take part in their rituals and ceremonies, they can only participate in nattu Gadhika.

 The converted people don't have belief in the rituals of the Adiya tribe, only for the death ritual, they will participate. Not only the converted people are going to church and worship Jesus, but others are also going to both church and temple and also using the cross. The conversion of Adiya people took place only at Varinilam colony, and the tendency is more in that colony because of the strong influence of tribal mission church.

Dressing Patterns: As the changes and influence of non-tribal people, market and advertisements they become very familiar with modern dresses. The traditional dress of Adiya female is known as chelakettu and it is worn by only elders know, during marriage and puberty ceremony some of them wear this but it is not compulsory now. Traditionally Adiya males are not allowed to cover the upper part of their body, they are only allowed to wear lungi or thorth (dhoti or towel). The end of slavery during the 80-90s changed the dress code of males; they started wearing shirt and dhoti. The changes didn't stop there, know the only few elder females are using the traditional chelakett others are wearing saree, salwar, churidar, jeans, t-shirt, etc. Not only the pattern of females the dress but also the pattern of males also changed from dhoti and shirt it changed to jeans, t-shirt, trousers, cargo pants etc. Most of them like to wear modern dresses than traditional dress. As the dress pattern changed the ornaments using also changed a lot, now they are using modern ornaments (fancy items) more, only elders are using traditional ornaments. The main reason for these changes is the influence of non-tribal people and market availability.

Administrations: Traditionally they only had tribal administration that governed by the Nattumoopan. But now the role of Nattumoopan become very less in their life, only he has power in rituals and ceremonies. The current administration in these colonies is the government administration like anywhere else in India. They are very happy with the government administration because it helped them to overcome slavery and poverty. Each colony is having oorukootam 4-5 times in a year other than Gram Sabah, with oorumoopan and tribal development officers. This meeting is only for scheduled tribes to say about their problems and discuss them with officials. Like any other non-tribes, they are having equal rights and opportunities everywhere. They are also participating in Gram Sabah. The shift from tribal administration to government administration made them more social, and it helped them to overcome the obstacles that restrict contact with the outer world. Because of democracy acculturation took place in their administrative setup and it becomes a reason for their change.

Health Care Systems: The health care of Adiya people also changed during the last 20 years, one of the major reason for the change in the health care system is the introduction of modern and allopathic medicine and the availability of medicines and facilities in the Manathavadi government hospital. They almost lost the knowledge about their ethnomedical practices in the past 10 years, because they had a belief that if they tell others about how to prepare the medicine, then the medicine will not work effectively, so they keep the preparation methods a secret. Their unwillingness to transfer the ethnomedicinal knowledge from one generation to another made them depend on modern medicinal practices, especially allopathic medicine. The former chief P K Kalan also has an important role in the shift of Adiya tribes from traditional medicine to allopathic medicine. He was the first chief who told them to follow allopathic medicine instead of believing in Gadhika. And they also lost the tradition of giving medicine while performing Gadhika for curing disease. Know the Adiya people prefer allopathic medicine to ethnomedicine and they are not having any Adiya shaman know. If allopathic medicine fails to cure the disease then they will try ayurvedic medicine, not their traditional ethnomedicine. People in the Varinilam colony will go to Kurichia shaman in the colony if the modern medicine fails, Kaithavally and Chekkot colony people prefer to go to Ayurveda hospital in Kattikulam (10 KM far from Thrissilery) if allopathic medicine fails. One of the main reason of this shift is that people lost the belief in their traditional medicine and its knowledge, now almost 98% of them likes allopathic medicine than traditional and ayurvedic medicine because of it helps in quick healing. They are having a government health centre almost

1 KM far from the colony, Asha worker from the health centre will visit each house in the colony twice or trice a week and will give necessary medicines and health advises to them. Other than the Asha worker each colony is having a helper known as Oorumitra, she helps the Asha worker in her work and also carries the diseased person to a health centre. Oorumitra of each colony is belonging to the Adiya tribe.

Language: The language of the Adiya tribe is known as Ravula Bhasha, it is a mixture of the languages Malayalam, Tamil and Kannada. Still, they are speaking Ravula bhasha at their home, but through the influence of non-tribes, they started to speak Malayalam. Through formal education, they learned English and Hindi. Some of them can speak Tamil because of the influence of Tamils in construction worksites.

SOURCES OF ACCULTURATION

Formal Education: While considering the sources of acculturation, formal education has an important role. Compulsory and free education up to the 10th standard and grants from the government helps Adiya children to go to school. Instead of this, they are having a jeep for children up to 10th standard to go to school and also breakfast at school. It leads them to cross the boundaries of their colony. They are getting an opportunity to go for higher education and thereby they can explore other cultures and modern trends outside the colony. Even though Adiya people are facing problems while going for higher education few of them are getting the opportunity to go for higher education. Formal education changed the traditional lifestyle of the Adiya youngsters and they started using modern dresses and other things because of the influence of non-tribes in the school and college. They are getting scientific knowledge and technological knowledge through formal education, which helps them to go for skilled labour. The shift from agricultural and unskilled labour skilled daily wage and company jobs are happened because of formal education. Know almost 40% of the youngsters of the colony are going for skilled labours. Some of them are going for government jobs and trying for government jobs, this trend is happened only because of the introduction of formal education to the colony.

Transportation and Communication: Transportation and communication have a very important role in the acculturation process of the Adiya tribe. Availability of two government public transportation buses through the Manathavadi- Anapara rout made easy transportation to the town, it helps them to access the nearest town and government hospital at Manathavadi (9 KM far). Other than this road there is a road connecting 3 colonies to the main road, and the road is enough for transportation in auto and jeep. Almost 20.5% of them are having a road to their house, others can easily access the road by walking less than 200 metres. The easy transportation facility in the colonies helps them to access the market and town easily, and it increased the rate of acculturation.

The use of mobile phones, television, radio and newspaper have also become the reason for acculturation among them. Youngsters of the colony are doing online shopping through Flipkart, Amazon, and Snapdeal because of the internet access in their smartphones. Not only mobile phones advertisements in television, newspaper, radio, and other social media networks like Facebook, WhatsApp also influences them.

Technology: Introduction of technology to the colony become another reason for acculturation, the smartphone has a key role in this. Youngsters of the colony are very familiar with the social networking sites like Whatsapp, Facebook and online shopping, video calling and TikTok etc. most of them spend their leisure time with a smartphone, they don't know about the traditional games. Availability of electricity helped with the technological adaptation of the Adiya people. Almost 76.92% of them are using television with DTH connection and some of them are using LED, LCD TV. TV becomes an important part of their daily life, almost 80% of the females in the colony spend their leisure time watching TV. They are using a bank account and ATM cards, youngsters of the colony are very familiar with ATM technology. Availability banking facility helps them for savings. Now they are trying to save money by using bank accounts, this trend is started before 4-5 years.

Market: Among Adiya tribes there is no tribal market; traditionally they had a habit of sharing things among them. Nowadays they depend on the common market in 'Pallikavala', 500 meters far from Chekkot colony and 1 KM from Kaithavally and Varinilam colony. Emergency things they will buy from the local shop near to the colony. But most of them prefer to buy things from the nearest town Manathavadi. Mostly male members of the house will go to Manathavadi for construction and other daily wage works while returning they will bring the household things. All family members including children will go to Manathavadi for shopping occasionally. They will get almost all the things in the Pallikavala market, but they prefer Manathavadi because of more options. Availability of different modern products in the Manathavadi accelerates the rate of acculturation. Now they are using aluminium and steel vessels instead of traditional mud pots, plastic and glass plates and glasses, new modern dresses instead of traditional dresses etc... And they are getting all new items in the town.

Credit Facilities

Kudumbashree: One of the important credit facility that helps almost 99% of the household is 'Kudumbashree', the women empowerment poverty eradication program, framed and enforced by the state poverty eradication mission of the government of Kerala in 1998. 9 ST Kudumbashree are there in 3 Adiya tribal colonies, and females having an age more than 18 is the members of each unit. Almost 98% of the females are part of the Kudumbasree unit. It gives them the facility to take loan once a year. The amount available for a loan will be the same for every member, and it will increase each year.

Informal Money Lenders: Another credit facility available in the colony is informal money lenders, they call them Annachi because they are from Tamil Nadu. They can take money up to 10000 from these informal money lenders with not less than 20% of interest. They have to return the money in weekly instalments. Most of the Adiya people are not taking a loan from banks because of lengthy procedures, and they only need less money that bank won't give a loan.

Church: Because of the influence of the church almost 10 families of the Varinilam colony is converted to Protestants. Christian missionaries helped Adiya people to overcome the after-effects of Naxalite movements and health problems because of imprisonment. And some of them converted to Christianity to overcome these problems.

Government Hospital: Availability of free medicines and check-up at the government hospital of Manathavadi becomes the key factor for the shift from ethnomedicine to allopathic medicine. They started to go to the hospital while pregnancy and for birth. Now there is no Adiya shaman and bethikarathi (midwife) in any of the colony.

Government Facilities: Electricity, bathroom, house, free rice are the main facilities that every Adiya families are getting from the government. These facilities changed the traditional house structure and infrastructure of the colony, and also the lifestyle. Almost 94.87% of Adiya families are having electricity. They got electricity an average of 15 years back. And the availability of electricity is very helpful for each one of them. It helps them to use different electronic appliances like mixer grinder, induction cooker, iron box, television, radio, mobile phone etc. and it became the major reason for acculturation among Adiya tribes. The traditional open pit is replaced by a closed latrine, almost 94.8% of Adiya households are having their bathroom facility, 30% of the bathrooms are tiled and having an Indian closet. Other facilities like grand for education, free tuition centre (Samoohya Padana Muri) etc. Also, have an important role in the acculturation of the Adiya tribe.

5
CONCLUSION AND RECOMMENDATION

The Adiya tribal communities are in the process of Detribalization with the impact of modernization. Their Cultural and Social, and Economic life factors are changing along with the changes happening around the world. Certain parts of culture, particularly relating to economic and technological is affected dramatically. Modernization has fortified the customary connections and bonds among them. Modern formal education, political organization, government administration, facilities, developmental programs, the influence of non-tribal population etc. are the notable reasons for acculturation within the Thrissilery village and Adiya communities there. Acculturation happened in almost all facets of their life, economic organization, political organization, dressing pattern, food habits and health care etc. As it should be the people's wish to preserve their tradition; no outsider has the right the force them to change them and force them to save their tradition. But, for greater wellness of the indigenous communities, we have to ensure all developments that happen in the culturally sensitive regions must follow measures of sustainability. In this case, we have to give more importance to sociocultural factors. Based on the extensive fieldwork following are the suggested recommendations particularly for this study area.

- A bottom-up model of development activities planning methods is needed to implement in Grama Panchayath to the State level.
- A sustainable model of developmental activity that protects tribal identities must be promoted.
- More field researches must be implemented by government or non-government agencies to understand real problems, needs and possible solutions on Adiya tribes of Kerala.
- Cultures and Traditions can be preserved through promoting performing and Non-performing arts like Gadhika dances for State Cultural centres and programs.
- A sustainable level of modernisation has to be identified and promoted in the tribal section as tribal identity is at threat.

REFERENCES

- Basu, S. K. Basu, SK: Health Status of Tribal Women in India. Social Change. 23 (4) Dec 1993. p. 19-39.
- Bhasin, V. (2007). "Status of tribal women in India". Studies on Home and Community Science, 1(1), 1-16.
- Bindu, B. (1998). "Socio-economic change among three Wayanad tribes. A study of Adiyan, Kattunaicken and Mullukuruman in eco-cultural context".(unpublished Ph. D thesis submitted to Calicut University, 1998).
- Bipul, Chandra Sarkar. (2017) "Impact of Modernisation on Economy of Tribal People Living in Dooars." International Journal of Research in Geography (IJRG), vol 3, no. 4, pp. 21-26. doi:http://dx.doi.org/10.20431/2454-8685.0304003
- Burman, B. R. (1983). "Transformation of tribes and analogous social formations". Economic and Political Weekly, 1172-1174.
- Census Report, 2011, Kerala State.
- Dube, S.C. (ed.) 1977. "Tribal Heritage of India". (Volume 1). Vikas: New Delhi.
- G P Gupta and Usha Singh (2007). "Changing Character of Tribal Environment : A Study of Saharia Landscape," ISBN 10: 8187445238 ISBN 13: 9788187445234.
- Gazetteer of India (1979), Kerala State, Trivandrum, Kerala History, vol i. Kerala BhAsha Institute, Ernakulam, op.cit, p.23 0.
- Gusfield, J. R. (1967). "Tradition and modernity: Misplaced polarities in the study of social change". American journal of sociology, 72(4), 351-362.
- Honderich, Ted (1995). The Oxford Companion to Philosophy. Oxford University Press. ISBN 978-0-19-866132-0.
- Jaganath Panday, (1981) "Tribal Peasantry Dynamics of Development", Inter India Publications, New Delhi. Pp-112-123.
- KC, Junaid (2018). "Re-Culture: The Contemporary Approach for Sustainable living". Scenario of Environmental Research and Development, ISBN: 978-93-5346-498-1 Page No. 169-174.
- Kumar, K. P. (2017). The Trajectory of Tribal Development Practice: The Case of Muthuvan Community in Kerala. Artha-Journal of Social Sciences, 16(2), 75-85.

- Kunhaman, M. (1989). "Development of Tribal economy". Classical Publishing Company.
- Kurup, A. M. (1971). "Status of Kerala Scheduled Tribes: A Study Based on Ethno-Demographic Data." Economic and Political Weekly, 1815-1820.
- Luiz, A.A.D. 1962. "Tribes of Kerala". New Delhi: Bharathiya Adimjathi Sevak Sang.
- Mandelbaum, D. G. (1941). Culture change among the Nilgiri tribes. American Anthropologist, 43(1), 19-26.
- Mitra, A., & Singh, P. (2008). "Trends in literacy rates and schooling among the scheduled tribe women in India". International Journal of Social Economics, 35(1/2), 99-110.
- Nidheesh, K. B. (2009). "Strengthening tribal communities through tribal womens self help groups in Kerala". International Journal of sociology and anthropology, 1(4), 077-081
- Ramachandran, B. (2004). "Transmutation of Economy and Transference of Status-A Case Study From Tribal Wayanad". Journal of Social Sciences, 9(1), 1-4.
- Sinha, D. (1963). The Role of the Phariya in Tribal Acculturation in a Central Indian Market. Ethnology, 2(2), 170-179. doi:10.2307/3772817
- Thomas A. Green (1997). "Folklore: an encyclopedia of beliefs, customs, tales, music, and art". ABC-CLIO. pp. 800–. ISBN 978-0-87436-986-1.
- William Logan, Malabar Manual (195 l), translation (Malayalam), "Logante Malabar Manual", T.V. Krishnan , Mathru Bhumi Publishers, Calicut, 1985, pp. 200 - 202.

APPENDICES

ABOUT THE AUTHORS

Junaid KC: a sociocultural anthropologist, and junior research fellow at the Center for Mountain Tourism and Hospitality Studies, HNB Garhwal Central University. His research interests focus on Social Entrepreneurship in tourism and Community-driven tourism planning. He holds a Master's degree in both Tourism Management and Anthropology from Pondicherry University. He is specialized in ethnography, Netnographic techniques and his research interest are focused on 'Tourism and Education/HRD'. He also has authored research papers in peer-reviewed journals and presented in international and national level conferences and seminars.

Divya NV: a sociocultural anthropologist, and junior research fellow at Department of Anthropology, HNB Garhwal Central University. She holds a Master's degree in Anthropology from Pondicherry University. Her research interests are focused on Community Based Tourism (CBT), Tourist Behavior, and Netnography. She has published research articles in UGC Care listed journals.